Changing The Leopard's Spots

Making Organizational Change Successful

Port R. Martin, Ed.D.

ISBN 1-4196-3238-8

To order additional copies, please contact us.
BookSurge
www.booksurge.com
1-866-308-6235
orders@booksurge.com

Dedication

To my wife Gayle, who makes me smile

Contents

Preface

It is a Biblical saying that one cannot change the spots on a leopard. Many would say that it is almost as difficult to make substantial changes to an organization. Yet, some organizations are more successful than others in meeting new challenges and adapting to times that demand important changes. They are representative of the leopard that *does* change his spots to thrive in his new environment. Perhaps this long considered piece of wisdom can be modified to meet new demands.

There are few leaders in any organization today who would argue that the pace of change is the same as it was one hundred years ago…or fifty years ago…or even a decade ago. Both private and public sector organizations are struggling to achieve desired results and stay close to the needs of their customers or constituents. Those who supply the capital that is the lifeblood for these organizations are asking for appropriate results, and modern information systems have given these financial sponsors a new ability to look over the shoulders of leaders at all levels.

Despite such approaches as Organizational Development, Total Quality Management, and Business Process Reengineering, research has shown that many (if not most) large-scale organizational changes achieve less than the final results desired. Chief executive officers, directors, governors, and even U.S. presidents come and go, often unable to turn the ship toward more desirable directions within the time deemed appropriate by those who have stakeholders' interests.

This book is designed to help leaders guide their organizations in directions that will make them more productive—given the resources they have at their disposal and the particular environmental changes they face.

Extensive research underlies the concepts discussed in this volume, and many of the sources are noted in the list of references at the end. However, the book is designed more for the practitioner of leadership than the scholar. It is hoped that knowledge contained herein will be of practical value to those who have real world problems to solve.

We will start with several chapters that provide a foundation upon which successful change efforts must be based. Leaders must understand what constitutes sound leadership and how important it is to the process of change. Those same leaders must understand the process of change and why humans seem to resist even the most positive of change efforts. Then, once a change is underway, it will be important to understand the collective resistance to change that is often imbedded in the culture. Once this background is understood, the leader and her organization can move forward by keeping in mind some critical and relatively straightforward concepts.

Chapter 6 will discuss—in relatively simple terms—the nature of the overlying problem that stops even the best intended changes in their tracks. Chapter 7 will move on to some simple ideas that can help to overcome the issues that block the implementation of change. The remainder of the book will provide guidance to make all the pieces come together.

There is really not much new in this volume except for the combination of elements leading to the final process. Scholars and practitioners alike will be familiar with many of the writers and researchers noted. What is unique is the combination of knowledge from a variety of fields, much of it over a half-century old. This book is not about brain surgery or flight to another planet; it is about changing organizations that exist today and which face today's problems.

The intent of the book is to make practitioners successful when they attempt significant organizational change. The words have been chosen carefully and most of them are relatively simple. An attempt has been made to extract relevant concepts from a variety of academic disciplines and then to integrate them into a practical whole. It is the author's hope that the reader will quickly grasp the ideas presented and then use them effectively in practice.

Changing

the

Leopard's

Spots

1

The Past

Human organizations have come quite a distance over the past 10,000 years or so. Where once small hunter-gatherer groups, families, and tribes were the norm, people have come together in ever-larger numbers to form entities that serve their collective purposes. Learning to farm crops and domesticate animals to provide steady food sources, our ancient ancestors began to develop at least a limited control over a physical environment that once dominated them completely.

Among the first major human civilizations, the Egyptians understood the need for planning and organizing their efforts. The building of the Pyramid of Cheops, covering 13 acres and composed of some

2,300,000 stone blocks of an average weight of about 2½ tons, required significant use of management techniques to oversee a total workforce estimated by some to exceed 100,000 workers.

Several thousand years ago the Chinese developed a very sophisticated governing bureaucracy that utilized concepts of organization, functional utility, efficiency and control that would be recognized today.

The Greeks conceived of management as an "art" and used the scientific method. Military and religious leaders established organizations that faced their respective environments with the intent of imposing their views on large groups of people.

The practices and challenges of today's business and community leaders that drive organizational changes are not as new as they might seem, but the environment has changed radically from the Egyptian pyramid-building days. The new changes, some subtle, require that the leader recognize the need for change and then be able to guide appropriate changes into being, quickly and effectively.

This sounds simple, but practice has shown it to be most challenging. It is estimated by some researchers that *over 70 percent* of major changes *do not achieve the results initially desired.* This can be most frustrating to the CEO who needs to meet the challenge of a competitor's new product or the state governor who must find a way to make fewer dollars go farther for a new fiscal year. Both will want changes that must be effected without unnecessary delays.

During the twentieth century the study of management and leadership progressed steadily, and the world learned more about itself as large organizations became more common. As the Industrial Age matured, men such as Frederick Winslow Taylor came forward with a variety of concepts and practices designed to make businesses more profitable. Taylor, as an example, applied his belief that tasks could be studied to the point that the most efficient methods could be identified. By then teaching these "best practices" to the labor force, businesses could more efficiently use their resources. This would, of course, lead to more profitable organizations and even increased benefits for those who performed the work.

Working with and following in Taylor's footsteps, Henry Gantt developed a charting method for tracking activities and the corresponding use of resources. Frank and Lillian Gilbreth continued to look at increasing the efficiency of organizations to include an early practical use of motion pictures to study work methods. About the same time Edwin Booz was establishing the beginnings of a consulting organization that would survive into the next century. (We will discuss consultants in a later chapter.)

Not surprisingly, the changes driven by the concepts of Frederick Taylor, known as Scientific Management, encountered significant resistance from the existing workforce, members of which were required to learn new techniques that significantly altered the manner of work. No longer did the worker individually decide how to do the work at hand. The job of management evolved into overseeing a workforce that should be conforming to standards set by efficiency experts who had identified the best methods.

The power of the individual worker or master craftsman now passed, in many instances, to the manager or foreman. An entire executive class of supervisors was born to oversee the new efficiencies.

This emphasis drove a strong focus on specifics of task accomplishment, overshadowing some of the previously dominant social aspects of doing work.

As the century progressed, a human relations movement began to study the importance of the human and social elements within organizations. Anchored by the Hawthorne Studies (1924-1932) of Elton Mayo and Fritz Roethlisberger, a new group of researchers sought to identify and test principles that would improve routine performance within the work environment while recognizing and evaluating the unique qualities that humans bring to an organization.

Just a little earlier than the Hawthorne Studies, Mary Parker Follett brought forward a variety of ideas that were not broadly recognized for their value until long after her death in 1933. She suggested that humans were largely social creatures, all of whom had knowledge which could be applied to building effective organizations—an important step toward participative management.

It was about this same time that Walter Shewart of Western Electric developed what would become known as Statistical Process Control (SPC), an application of statistics to quality control that helped his company dramatically reduce the number of items rejected during manufacturing processes.

His colleague, Edwards Deming, later incorporated this concept into work he did for the United States War Department during World War II and subsequently for post-war Japan. Deming's success in helping war-torn Japan grow into an economic powerhouse several decades later eventually grew into a concept known as Total Quality Management (TQM). Adopted by many organizations seeking quality improvements in the 1980s, the fourteen principles espoused by Deming in TQM were an attempt to balance quantitative methods with the human environment to improve overall organizational performance.

World War II brought many of the ideas developed in private industry into support of the national effort to win the war. Alfred Sloan, Henry Ford, Chester Barnard and others brought their ideas and experience to the public sector and demonstrated the universality of many of the management theories.

Paralleling these developments were useful advancements in the field of psychology. Carl Jung's work in the area of psychological types was blended into a practical application by Isabel Myers and Katheryn Briggs. The Myers-Briggs Type Indicator provided a means of examining human performance in light of natural tendencies toward particular combinations of behaviors. Familiarity with the sixteen basic types could assist in establishing the most appropriate means for human interactions between supervisors, subordinates, and peers, thereby improving human work performance.

Abraham Maslow developed his Hierarchy of Needs that established a sense of human priorities when dealing with a given person's environment. Kurt Lewin, who left Germany for the United States in 1932, developed a variety of theories regarding social aspects of organizations, which helped to build the foundations of what would become known as Organizational Development (OD). He believed that human behavior was a product of both the individual and the environment, and he made significant contributions to the concepts of group theory, feedback, and resistance to change.

As new ideas touching on human behavior were developed, a few researchers began to pull the various pieces together. Douglas McGregor proposed that the manner in which a manager viewed his subordinates would guide his style of working with those subordinates. Theory X, where people are viewed as immature, self-centered, and disloyal to corporate goals, would demand a strict, controlling work environment to achieve the company's mission. On the opposite end of the scale, Theory Y, where people are viewed with respect as being worthy of trust and confidence, would dictate a very open and participative environment for best results.

Frederick Herzberg studied the motivation of employees and divided work factors into two general areas: those that were necessary but not motivating (hygiene) factors and those that helped to improve (motivate) human performance in the workplace. For the leader who wished to encourage new behaviors of followers, this was very important to know.

Research by Robert Blake and Jane Mouton led to their development of The Managerial Grid, a method for examining the balance between a focus on tasks or on human relationships. Their view actually illuminated an existing tension between people and their work that had been ongoing as various approaches to management and leadership developed.

In parallel the concept of Organizational Development emerged from the human relations research during the middle part of the twentieth century. This process—which incorporated data gathering and analysis, feedback to the organization, and facilitation to guide the development of new solutions—was to be among the first large-scale intervention systems employed by organizations and their consultants to guide significant organizational changes.

OD was followed in the 1980s by a focus on methods developed by Edwards Deming known as Total Quality Management, an approach designed to assist organizations in improving the quality of their products and services. As this approach began to lose favor in the early 1990s, Business Process Reengineering (BPR) entered the mix of tools that attempted to address organizational change needs. Governmental, industrial, military, and non-profit organizations began reinventing themselves with regularity.

Even though considerable resources were devoted to these change efforts, one aspect remained puzzling: the lack of routine, long-term success stories in spite of some impressive individual cases that were serving as models. Consistent successes were somewhat rare. While much value in adapting to meet new challenges was often seen by organizational leaders, many became cautious when asked to commit significant time and financial resources to support new change efforts.

Looking at the growth of concepts that occurred largely in the twentieth century, several themes emerged:

- Work is a balance of social and task aspects.
- Many ideas are further developments of previously suggested concepts.
- Individual methods can be valuable if applied in the environments for which they are most applicable.
- Leaders must understand how to apply those methods best fitting their particular situations.

> A leader's effort to change the leopard's spots must be selective in choosing the most appropriate method(s) to do so.

2

Leadership: What is It?

Leadership has been present in human groups (or even pairs) as long as one individual desired to have another do something that he wanted done, perhaps in a certain way. History books are filled with stories of kings and queens, generals and admirals, religious leaders and others who have significantly helped to set the directions for their dominions.

With the steadily increasing presence of democratic governments, elected representatives have been chosen by political bodies to represent various collections of people. Business organizations have begun to look at their senior executives as leaders in much the same sense that politicians might look at their legislative head or president. It is these leaders who will be guiding changes, successful or not, as organizations adapt to their new environments.

Joseph Rost's book *Leadership for the Twenty-First Century* traces an interesting history of the word **leadership**. He noted that the word *lead* first appeared in dictionaries in the eighteenth century and appeared to mean "to guide" or "to go first." A leader, then, would be someone who performed such an act. The comprehensive Century Dictionary (1889-1911) then defined leadership simply as "[t]he office of a leader; guidance; control." Rost noted a variety of other definitions of both leader and leadership before revealing his own definition, which will serve this discussion well. He defined leadership as follows:

> "**Leadership** is an *influence relationship* among *leaders and followers* who *intend real changes* that reflect their *mutual purposes*."

As the words in italics (added to his definition) indicate, the term leadership can be thought to be composed of four key elements:

- It is an influence (as opposed to a command) relationship.

- Its environment includes people within which some are considered leaders and others followers.
- The participants in this relationship intend real changes.
- The intended changes are for some mutual purpose or benefit.

Common sense would argue that leaders have participated actively in human organizations from the first gatherings of humans on the earth. However, the study of leadership as a topic, separate from its complementary cousin management, has been slow to occur.

As commonly as leadership can be identified as a key factor in the history of the world, often surrounding events recalling military triumphs and failures, the routine training of military organizations so as to develop excellent leadership performance is relatively new. The U.S. Navy, as an example, did not begin requiring leadership training of all its members at specific career milestones until the late 1980s, ordered then by Vice Admiral Michael Boorda (later to be the Chief of Naval Operations) when he was serving as the Chief of Naval Personnel.

In the business world the term *management* has often been thought to incorporate the term *leadership* as an included element rather than as a separate or complementary term. (In many schools of business this belief continues to this day.) Such was the influence of Frederick Winslow Taylor's Scientific Management in changing the way many organizations looked at the accomplishment of work that the term *management* was applied to all circumstances where work was overseen by some supervisory authority who was not necessarily a master craftsman (as was often the case in preceding times). Only toward the end of the twentieth century did scholars start to make a clear distinction between the terms and the functions that they described regarding the guidance of work in organizations. Over time, efficiency would become the manager's primary standard.

In the current sense, managers would be commonly described as supervising the accomplishment of work in selecting the most efficient manner to achieve the goals of the organization of which they are a part. Using Taylor's guidance, they would look for the best methods to do the work and then ensure that their subordinates used these identified techniques and procedures. High quality managers can be very effective in a static environment as they refine the work methods to be ever more efficient.

Looking at personality types (as defined by Myers-Briggs), one might assume that individuals testing high in characteristics representative of those who have a *sensing* preference would tend to be superior managers. They are practical, based in the present and likely to rely heavily on facts—facts made known to them via their five senses. They are likely to notice and respond to events that have actually occurred or are in the process of happening rather than to look at things that might happen in the future. With this type of orientation they would most likely perform best when in a relatively stable environment that is well grounded on facts. In organizations this would translate into a focus on existing processes and procedures in a well-defined organizational structure.

Organizations need managers to keep the workers performing efficiently and to handle the present day's challenges. So who looks toward tomorrow? It would be the leader who is interested in doing something differently in response to anticipated changes in the environment. This might well be the world of those with an *intuitive* preference in personality type. This is not to say that sensing individuals are doomed to be managers and only intuitive people can lead, only that characteristics of those personality types may make them more effective at some activities than at others.

The leader, by definition, is doing something that is different, something that has not necessarily been done before. The *intuitive* person lives in a future-based world, often thinking of "what might be" rather than "what exists now." This focus on the future invites a reliance on hunches, visions, and new ideas. One might logically assume that the *intuitive* person would be more comfortable in a leadership role than the *sensing* one. It is the nature of the leader to envision a new state and then to convince others to follow on a path to that new end state. This, then, is the practical illustration of the Rost definition.

The leader is, by definition, doing something different, something that has not necessarily been done before.

This discussion of the intuitive versus the sensing individuals might be interpreted as supporting the argument that leaders are born, not made. (This is only partially true.) While many characteristics (to include aspects of personality types) are inherited from our parents, many other factors impact on the development of leaders and their abilities to practice the craft in a real situation.

One must look at the personality aspects of intuition and sensing as opposite ends of a continuum. Almost all of us will fall somewhere in the middle, a unique combination of both viewpoints. In some situations we will exhibit the characteristics of the intuitive and in others our sensing characteristics will dominate. However, we will have a preference in those situations. Leaders must be aware of their own (and their subordinates') tendencies to most effectively accomplish new things.

Effective leaders have the ability to recognize new states of an organization and, hopefully, to see at least a rough pathway leading to the desired new condition. This is the "vision" so often discussed in changing organizations. It is only the first step as per the definition of leadership. Next the leader must convince others (the followers) that the vision is sound, that it can be achieved, and that it is advantageous to accomplish. The sense of mutuality must be built between the vision of the leader and the expectations of the followers. If the benefits of the new state do not outweigh the negative aspects, it will be difficult to exercise leadership to achieve the change. Perhaps directive actions will force the changes necessary, but leadership in its purest sense will not be utilized.

It must be noted that *perception* is a critical aspect in building the consensus that the effective leader desires. Each of us can only experience the immediate world through our five senses. The signals these senses send to our brain are then processed through an incredibly complex process that matches our current perceptions to other aspects recorded in our memory. The conclusions that we draw from this analysis drives our perception of the world around us at any given moment. This argues that with a population of six billion people (or more) living on this planet, there are six billion perceptions of the reality of any situation. Even when many of us are in agreement, we do not see a given situation in the exact same manner.

One of the challenges of leadership is to guide the perceptions of followers in such a way that the vision of the leader becomes a practical reality for the followers. They must see the value in achieving the organizational goals in a manner that allows them to accept the work needed to achieve them as aligned with their own personal beliefs, goals, and directions. This drives the mutuality expressed in the Rost definition. One example may clarify what this can mean, and it is an example of leadership under the most difficult of situations—leadership in combat.

Regarding the military, a common conception would be the coordination of human actions under horrific conditions where even the slightest mistake or hesitation might bring death to one or more of the participants. The military has a very well-established chain of command, dictating senior-subordinate relationships. The seniors are often pictured as directing juniors to accomplish tasks, many at great risk to the subordinate (as well as the senior) and other participants. A senior member may point, yell orders or in some other manner indicate what must be done. This "directiveness" may appear to reflect something other than an influence relationship, but it actually takes into account a prior agreement to work together.

Military units routinely practice under more benign conditions than the actual combat tasks they will face. In a training situation the combat team works together, develops coordination, and practices skills under conditions that are designed to simulate the conditions they will face later. Ideally, leaders and followers develop a faith in each other that allows followers to accept the directions from their seniors as reflecting their mutual benefit. They are establishing a relationship where the apparent directions of a senior automatically reflect their mutual desires to successfully complete the assigned mission. What is often termed as esprit-de-corps or morale is a reflection of the degree of bonding that these soldiers have achieved.

This type of relationship is built on trust. It is built on a bedrock of trust in the leader's ability to make the correct decisions. And it is achievable in other than military organizations.

In their book *Credibility: How Leaders Gain and Lose It, Why People Demand It*, James Kouzes and Barry Posner report on their research as to the most critical attributes that followers expect in their leaders. In 1993 their surveys showed the top four characteristics to be honesty (87%), forward-looking (71%), inspiring (68%), and competent (58%), many of the same qualities that are developed in the military training model. In particular Kouzes and Posner have consistently found that three of those attributes—honesty, competence and inspiration—form the nucleus of what can be termed *credibility*. Interestingly, the term credibility itself has as its root the Latin verb *credere*, to believe. In establishing the leadership relationship with followers, then, the leader must become believable to the followers. Trust in the leader then forms when credibility is established.

In connecting back to Joseph Rost's definition, the leader proves believable to the follower who then trusts the leader's judgment as to the mutuality of tasks to be performed. The *intuitive* preference possessed by some individuals may help to provide the forward-looking aspect to include the ability to envision a new state and to define it for others. However, those with a *sensing* preference can still take advantage of this aspect if they are aware of the value and differences of these preferences. As an example, developing a particular vision or solution may demand that another person help to provide the vision that may be slow in coming naturally to the sensing leader. The *intuitive* assistant may be invaluable in this role.

In addition, it is necessary to keep in mind that it is the *perception* of the follower that defines the strength of the relationship. If the follower trusts and finds the leader credible, he is more likely to find a mutuality in purpose as defined by the leader's actions and directions. If the follower perceives that he cannot trust the judgment of the appointed leader, the relationship may well lack the mutuality that Rost emphasizes in his definition.

> It is the *perception* of the *follower* that defines the strength of the leader-follower relationship.

We have not discussed one key aspect of this leader-follower relationship: change. The manager seeks to make the organization more *efficient*, but the leader wants to make it more *effective*. The manager wants to adjust the existing organization; the leader wants something different. It may be a matter of magnitude, but it is a significant difference.

Before the appearance of the leopard can be modified, a leader must decide that there is a need for change and then envision the new state. Once this is done, she must convince others, the followers, that they must modify their behaviors to achieve this new goal. But before we can proceed, we must take a careful look at change, and changing, if we are to understand the essence of the problem of seeking and achieving a new, improved level of performance in an organization…or changing the spots on a leopard.

3

Change and Changing

Change as a noun is defined as an alteration or modification. It involves a transition from one state, condition or phase to another. As a verb it means to cause to be different or to alter. Simply stated, something is going to be different when the change is completed. Duplicating the present will not effect change so something must be done differently. In a given environment you cannot expect to do more of the same and significantly change the nature of the final results.

Most of us are involved in a constant stream of small changes from the moment we awake until the day is finished. Our environment is slightly different every day so we dress differently, eat differently and accomplish different activities to achieve needed results. But we also establish a set of norms—rules of thumb—assisting us to accomplish those changing tasks, that provide a consistent framework for the needed changes. Working at a Wall Street firm defines a wardrobe appropriate to that environment; going to the beach has a different set of requirements. For an average day we consciously limit the number of options that we need to consider so that we can efficiently dress, eat, work, and play with a minimum of planning and discussion. Because of the limitations of the human brain, these steps to simplify routine decision making are invaluable in allowing our cognitive abilities to focus on the most important issues at the present time.

When we move toward larger and more expansive changes, such as a move across the country or to a site beyond the national borders, we spend more time getting ready for the change and planning the specific steps. It can be a time of great stress to go with both positive and negative feelings. For the moment we do not have the comfort of a set routine, and we must spend considerable energy monitoring our progress and the results of our actions.

These same elementary actions and emotions apply to changing organizations. Organizations are collections of people, and they change *one person at a time*. Many people may change in a short period of time, but they still do it individually. As in any collection of individuals, some do it well, some do it poorly, and some achieve a moderate degree of success between the extremes. Any change plans must reflect that humans will be involved, and this very fact can play havoc with any logical, rational change planning.

Organizations are collections of people, and they change one person at a time.

We will keep coming back to the important issue of *perception* when interpreting the impact of change on individuals. Exactly the same happening or event will be seen in a slightly different light by every human observer. There may be some general agreement as to what has happened, but each person will evaluate the event in light of her existing knowledge as reflected by such individual aspects as experience, culture, genetics, personality type, education, financial security, skill development, physical location, ethnic background, and a host of other influences.

Our response to a given change or series of changes will reflect this individualized perception of the event in question. It will also align with our anticipation of the given outcome of the event, predictability being the preferred state. If we understand the nature of the change and feel we can personally guide the results in a desirable direction, we will be much more comfortable with the given situation. Interestingly, even *bad* results may be moderately acceptable if we can predict them; we humans feel particularly threatened when we feel we will be impacted by something that we do not understand.

To address problems of a significant nature, we establish correspondingly important systems to provide this needed structure. We establish nations and governments so that we can construct a set of rules to govern our routine transactions. We know what most of the cars on the road will be doing most of the time—in the United States they stay on the right side of the road and stop at stoplights that turn red. In general, we are comfortable with these routines, and we have systems in place to enforce the rules.

Some of these needs to establish boundaries of behavior can be connected to the hierarchy of needs proposed by psychologist Abraham Maslow. He established a hierarchy of basic needs that starts at the lowest level with physiological needs underlying the next higher safety needs. Above them he listed love (social) needs, esteem needs, and then, at the top, a need for self-actualization. He felt that a significant lack of a lower level need would draw a person toward a focus on the lower need to the exclusion of higher level needs.

For instance, the need of the human body for food on a regular basis would naturally dominate the thinking of a starving man. Thoughts of social or esteem needs would not be regarded as particularly important. If the body does not survive, the other needs are largely irrelevant. The next higher level, safety, helps to guarantee that the basic physiological needs are met over the long term, again helping the human to remain strong within its environment.

This begins to connect with the issue of change when we start to look at the progression of humans from the earliest days of walking upright to the present. Most living things have adapted to their environments to ensure both their present and long-term needs are met, ensuring the survival of the species. Those that cannot adapt as changes occur become extinct.

Using superior cognitive abilities, however, humans have gradually taken more and more control over their environment rather than follow the dictates of weather, geography, and other threats to survival. This has led to a human expectation that most things can be controlled to ensure long-term survivability, meeting the two lowest levels of Maslow's hierarchy. This expectation, then, may convince many of us that changes are new threats to our environment, threats that must be mastered.

This recognition of change as a new environmental challenge then causes many to look for a solution that restores a former balance of forces. The more things change, the more we feel a loss of control. The magnitude of change, therefore, is related to *our perception* of a loss of control. The same change will affect each of us in a slightly different manner. A change is minor if we believe it is; a change is important if we regard it as such. Individual perceptions will then drive our emotional and cognitive responses.

The magnitude of change is related to our *perception* of a loss of control over our immediate environment.

Understanding these basic aspects of change is important as an underlying foundation for anticipating and effectively resolving resistance to change. All leaders need to recognize that these human needs must be addressed in any forthcoming change effort in a manner that is appropriate for the leaders and followers involved.

In 1966 Warren Bennis, in his book *Changing Organizations*, stated that the theories of social change then in existence were "theories suitable only for observers of social change, not theories for participants in, or practitioners of, social change. They are theories of *change* and not theories of *changing*." It would seem that Bennis' thought is largely true today if our lack of success in changing organizations is an appropriate measure.

As an example of a *theory of change*, Kurt Lewin introduced a very simple model. He described three stages that the change would require:

- Unfreeze the organization;

- Install the new behaviors;
- Refreeze the organization.

First, the organization needed to be unfrozen, made ready and open to the new changes. This could be achieved by a variety of methods that made the need for change apparent to those who would need to modify their behaviors. Workshops, as an example, could help people examine the present state of affairs and come to a conclusion that change was necessary.

Once open to change, the organizational leaders, often with the help of trained consultants, could then assist in training participants to take on the behaviors that reflected the needed changes. Once everyone had been properly trained, the organization could enter a stable environment once more. It would be "refrozen."

Although this simple model probably does reflect three general phases descriptive of organizational change, it may oversimplify the actions needed to finalize the change. Unfreezing the organization can be effectively done through awareness development, but the next two steps are much more difficult to achieve.

This Organizational Development approach often finds it difficult to train each individual with exactly the right behaviors as the training is, once again, subject to individual perceptions and interpretations. Training an entire organization to act differently takes time, and the internal and external environments do not stop changing. This leads to a difficulty in finishing the training and then refreezing the organization. The genie is out of the bottle and probably will not return, at least not soon.

The first step to establishing a *theory of changing* may well be to take careful note of the theories of change, but then we must move on to the action position of effecting change—*changing*. We must recognize that change and changing are not the same thing. We must remember that change is individual and *perceived* differently *by each individual*. Something will soon be different, and leaders will be guiding the followers to some mutual goal.

To understand fully the reason why many of these individuals will resist changes, even if they appear to be beneficial to the leader, we must examine the phenomenon of resistance to change. For some reason the leopard would prefer the present set of spots.

We must remember that change is individual and perceived differently by each human being.

4

Resistance to Change

Resistance to change can take many forms. It may be subtle and relatively invisible or it may be loud and quite visible to the naked eye. Some individuals will express their emotions in the form of anger or frustration. Others will silently try to manage the stress and may suffer a variety of human ailments. An entire organization may on the surface tolerate a leader's actions to drive home a change only to completely reverse course once the leader is no longer physically present.

What, then, can the leader of an organization do to make needed changes more acceptable to the followers—to develop the mutual purposes that are needed? How can he address resistance to change so that its effect will not fatally disrupt the changing process?

The first step for a leader interested in effecting successful changes is to understand the very nature of resistance to change and to understand that it is a naturally occurring phenomenon, one likely to appear in any organization at any time. Simply stated, resistance to change is:

- distinctly individual in nature;
- deeply rooted psychologically;
- neither rational nor necessarily predictable;
- and naturally occurring.

These four aspects hold the key to developing solutions that will minimize the negative aspects that resistance to change can inject into a seemingly well-developed change plan.

We know that each human being has a brain that interacts with the environment using the five senses as interpreted in light of previously acquired information. The perceptions of each individual will then be slightly different, leading to a somewhat unique response to each situation. When it comes to evaluating an organizational change, each human participant will quickly, and almost instinctively, interpret the events in relation to his individual situation—previous experiences with similar occurrences, present needs (again Maslow appears), and a variety of current and long-term priorities. Such simple and common events as a poor night's sleep before engaging a set of changes for the first time may significantly impact on the acceptability of the changes for a specific individual.

Responses to a given change may then appear to be totally irrational, because specific individuals are interpreting the impact of the change using their own perceptions and interpretations to guide their reactions. These responses may appear to be entirely illogical based on the assumptions of the planners, but they reflect the human aspects of the people who are most affected by the changes.

The individuals and groups who do most of the regular work of the organization are very likely to feel a loss of control of their immediate environment when they are directed to make substantial changes, *substantial* being in the eye of the beholder. Having to deal with a threat to the control of their immediate environment, their security need, they respond in myriad ways.

There will be some organizational members who are ready for the changes at hand and will welcome them enthusiastically. Their personality type may help them adjust quickly to new things and ways of doing business. They may see the need for change and see personal value in making it effective. These people are willing allies of the organization's leaders and can be of great assistance to the change agents leading the effort. They can help their associates interpret changes with a credibility that may not exist outside an immediate work group.

Most of the humans in an organization, however, will struggle with an interpretation of the changes proposed and not fully understand their personal impact. This lack of understanding will cause each individual to make assumptions to develop what he or she *perceives* to be a complete understanding of the situation. These assumptions will fill in the unknowns with the personal expectations of each individual. For the leader facing this potential resistance, it is important to know that many of these assumptions being made will be in light of a "worst possible case" scenario so that the individual concerned can take action to prevent the worst from happening.

Some participants will have seen organizational changes of a similar nature before, and they will assume that the results of the current process may mirror those of their past experiences. Others will see the changes as a threat to their jobs and begin the process of fortifying their current position or looking elsewhere for new employment opportunities. Some will evaluate retirement, and others will experience stress to such a degree that it will affect their ability to function, possibly leading to physical illnesses. Responses may be either overt in open defiance of the changes or covert, hidden in the day-to-day actions that can sabotage the change effort very quietly.

The following story regarding a common change opportunity may serve as an example. In an annual look at the organization, the senior leaders have decided to move some boxes on an organization chart so that functions are better organized in relation to their view of the processes that support the daily execution of their business.

Two women, close friends who have worked together for many years and whose desks sat side-by-side, will now be working in separate buildings. Over the years, these employees have become close friends on both a work and social basis. They routinely carpool, attend the events where their children are participants and share many aspects of their lives. The proximity of their desks has also assisted them in their work as they routinely have shared their workloads so that neither of them is overwhelmed during a crisis. The new arrangement, putting one of the women physically closer to the managers she often supports, has been designed to improve efficiency. This simple organizational change has not been perceived favorably by the two employees.

Suddenly life is different. Although the working environments appear to be benign and even cheerful, the sudden disruption of a routine developed over many years has an impact. Supervisors note that both women's productivity has decreased, and crises seem to occur regularly with associated overtime costs. One of the women has developed a medical problem that requires many hours of sick time attending doctor's appointments. The other seems more sullen and is unlikely to volunteer to assist others in her immediate work area. Carpools are now out of the question as work hours for the two women are not compatible. Although neither has shown overt resistance to the changes, the two former office mates also show no real support for the change.

This is a short story about two members of an organization. If the change also involves 150 other "minor" organizational adjustments, the collective resistance to change, loss of productivity, and related personnel costs might well make the leaders rethink their change proposals. Sometimes it is cost effective to have a couple of the boxes on the organization chart slightly out of position as long as the work is effectively completed.

This tale also demonstrates how seemingly minor organizational adjustments can have very significant impacts on overall corporate performance. Employee health costs are a growing issue and have costs reflected in both performance and profitability. In an organization consisting of hundreds of small work teams, the losses in effectiveness and efficiency are multiplied many times over. The cost of change goes way beyond acquisition of new furniture, computers or company letterhead. These costs are associated strongly with humans and their "natural" resistance to change—their perceptions that they have lost control over their immediate environments.

> Seemingly minor organizational adjustments can have very significant impacts on overall corporate performance.

The members of any organization develop a collection of behaviors that they believe will make them successful in that organization. Over time these behaviors represent a routine that reflects how the business of the organization is conducted. To change these routine behaviors and address the aspects that lead to resistance to change, leaders must understand more about these collective behaviors—about the organization's culture.

The task for adjusting the leopard's spots must take into account more than individual resistance to change. We must examine the entire culture within which the leopard resides.

5

Organizational Culture

Resistance to change is a unique and somewhat individual phenomenon, but what happens when it appears to come from the organization as a whole? Leaders are often tasked with the changing of organizational directions that affect large numbers of people. To address this "large" aspect, we must examine and better understand the concept of culture, and, more specifically, *organizational culture*.

For a start at understanding this aspect of an organization, *The American Heritage Dictionary* would have us believe that culture is "[t]he totality of socially transmitted behavior patterns, arts, beliefs, institutions, and all other products of human work and thought characteristic of a community or population." This is a good start as the reader can easily see that an organization would qualify as a community or population of people drawn together to accomplish the goals of that entity.

For the purposes of this discussion, however, it would be best for us to settle on a definition that is closely tied to the organizations that we encounter on a regular basis. For this purpose, let us turn to Edgar Schein, one of the founders of the field of organizational psychology. His book, *Organizational Culture and Leadership* (2nd Ed.), defines culture as:

> "A pattern of shared basic assumptions that the group learned as it solved its problems of external adaptation and internal integration, that has worked well enough to be considered valid and, therefore, to be taught to new members as the correct way to perceive, think, and feel in relation to those problems."

This definition allows a more organizational focus and infers that the behaviors that currently help define a group were developed mutually as the collection of individuals solved problems together. The culture, as it were, now reflects a collection of the successful habits that the group finds helpful in accomplishing organizational tasks. These habits are then taught to new members so that they will act in the *proper* and *most effective* manner as defined by the collective will.

From this definition one should infer that the organizational culture did not form overnight; it developed over a period of time as the group members worked to refine their methods. What was determined to be *mutually* satisfactory was retained, and ineffective or undesirable behaviors were minimized or eliminated entirely. The degree to which individuals and groups enforce these behaviors would tend to determine the strength of the culture thus formed. The *sense of mutuality* may help to demonstrate the value of leadership in establishing a culture and definitely provides a definitional link to our original discussion of leadership.

To many readers, however, culture probably remains a vague term that defines a rather loose collection of things that totally define a group. It has the aura of a fog bank—large, all-encompassing and somewhat difficult to describe or define precisely. Yet it can have very visible aspects that can be evaluated by some survey-type instruments.

I would ask the reader to think for a moment of a time when he or she was a new member of an organization. That organization could be any church, sports team, or work group. As you walked around, somewhat amazed by your new environment, perhaps you started to do something that had been common to your past. Very gently, a more experienced member of the group, certainly a more acculturated one, tugged on your sleeve and whispered in your ear, "We don't do it that way around here. Let me show you how it's done." You have just encountered the culture doing its best to show you the proper behaviors, methods to be successful in your new culture.

If a culture forms so as to choose the most effective behaviors for everyday organizational life, what happens to that culture when it must change—or more precisely, when the people must change? Suddenly there is a challenge to the established way of doing things. Behaviors must be adjusted. New steps must be taught to new members—and to old ones. But should we step too quickly away from those things that have made us successful in the past? Many would think not. The culture, developed to support success, will question the need for new behaviors.

It is not hard to see that the culture itself will naturally act as a brake for the change process, wanting to evaluate past methods in light of new ones. This is not a process that can be achieved instantaneously, no matter how much effort is exerted by the organization's leaders. Since cultures often take years to develop fully, it is not wise to expect them to change quickly in spite of a serious crisis as perceived by the leaders.

If a culture is to change, leaders must be aware of the existing one so that any changes can be properly directed toward adjusting established behaviors in such a way that the new state can be achieved. This is not as difficult as it may sound as a culture can be viewed in light of the values held by the organization's members, particularly the priority given to the major values held in common. These values, are of two types: *cultural* and *operational*.

Cultural values help to define the very organization itself, connecting deeply with the qualities that are most important. They will form as the group first comes together and will often be very difficult to change. They help to define the balance between the social or relational aspects of the organization and the tasks that must be accomplished. This aspect reflects a tension earlier defined by Robert Blake and Jane Mouton as described in *The Managerial Grid*, a discussion of how managerial style will vary as emphasis achieves a balance between the need for relationships and the need for task achievement.

> Cultural values help to define the very heart of the organization, connecting deeply with the qualities that are held most dear.

Some examples of cultural values of the relationship variety might include customer satisfaction, employee empowerment, leadership, teamwork, and family involvement. Task-related values might include firm management control, efficient use of resources, maximizing profitability, and emphasizing high-quality products.

The cultural values are deeply embedded in the organization and may not be as readily apparent to the casual observer as the operational values. Operational values, in contrast, reflect the manner in which the organization does business every day. Some of these values will reflect the effectiveness of actions that the organization must accomplish on a regular basis. They could include creativity, high motivation, utilization of power, and risk-taking. Other values such as compassion, cooperation, and loyalty may reflect the ethical or correctness of actions.

Instruments that can identify the embedded priorities of these two sets of values will allow an organization to define the culture that exists and even establish the defining values of a new culture, one more appropriate to supporting the changes that are planned.

As an example, a culture that is highly disciplined, focused on profitability, and married to tradition is quite different from one that emphasizes customer relationships, family, and creativity. Either culture might be correct for a given situation, but they are obviously going to be different. Leaders need to know what their existing culture is, decide on the correct new culture, and then chart a course to build the new one.

Dorine Andrews and Susan Stalick (*Business Reengineering: The Survival Guide*) approach the business reengineering problem by looking at an organization as composed of three layers: a physical/technical layer, an infrastructure layer, and a value layer. The value layer would represent the aspects that define the very nature of the organization. From those values an infrastructure would develop to reflect the management and reward systems that would support the daily operations of the organization. The top and most visible layer would then be defined by the processes, organization structure, and technologies needed to accomplish the routine tasks of the organization.

By looking at organizations in this manner, it becomes apparent that changing the performance will require more than a simple modification of a process or two. It becomes necessary to ensure that the infrastructure is appropriate to support the changes in processes or structure, and that the new organizational features and underlying cultural values are in alignment. Should any of the aspects not work well together, the organization would have a tendency to support changes that are more closely attuned to the underlying values and resist those that are further removed. Hence, resistance to change would emerge to hinder the behavioral modifications desired.

John Kotter and James Heskett (*Corporate Culture and Performance*) have looked further into the influence of this corporate culture aspect to help define practical aspects for leaders to keep in mind. They note that founders of organizations can help create performance-enhancing cultures early in a firm's life. The behaviors that they encourage and reward *from the first days* will help to determine success. As time progresses, the daily routines that are linked to success will be reinforced by the organization's structure and reward systems, helping the most productive behaviors to become embedded in the culture.

It must be noted that strong cultures do not always lead to success. Strong cultures do reinforce behaviors as defined by that organization, but if they are inappropriate to the internal or external environments, they will not necessarily lead to excellent organizational performance. Kotter and Hescutt go on to emphasize that organizations that do perform well over a significant period of time also value the ability to change, to adapt to changing conditions.

So, what is the value of this discussion of organizational culture? It is the recognition that individuals in organizations collectively hold some values very dear. When behavioral changes are desired on a permanent basis, the collective aspect of an organization must be considered. The collective response to change, defined within the culture, must be addressed to create lasting change.

Individuals change one person at a time at a pace defined by each one of them. Organizations change when they reorder their values to meet the *perceived* changes in the environment. In summary, both the individual and collective change aspects must be addressed in any change strategy.

The collective response to change, defined within the culture, must be addressed to create lasting change.

6

The Problem

Leading successful organizational change requires that leaders and followers establish their mutual purposes to accomplish something new. On the surface it might seem to be a relatively simple task to establish a plan that is credible in the eyes of the followers, thereby establishing the support necessary to effect the needed changes. It is not quite that simple.

There are several models that organizational theorists have advanced to provide guidance toward establishing concrete steps necessary to accomplish a given change. The generally stated steps listed by A.O. Manzini in *Organizational Diagnosis: A Practical Approach to Company Problem Solving and Growth* are typical of the change process models. He listed the following steps:

- Perception of crisis
- Gathering of data
- Diagnosis of problem
- Planning
- Plan implementation
- Evaluation
- Plan modification

These steps appear to be a very solid and rational approach to tackling any organizational problem, although some may not be critical to a specific effort. In fact, many organizational members might say that they have seen a process very similar to this in action recently in their organizations. The books are filled with versions of this step-by-step methodology—books of both an academic and practitioner nature. What we need to keep in mind is that as many as 70% of change efforts are not judged as fully successful. Still, we insist that these are the steps to follow.

This step-by-step methodology is an engineering approach to problem solving. Why would that be important to note? It is important, because engineers and their processes have had some highly visible successes over the past several centuries that followed this rational, linear approach to successful conclusions. Bridges have spanned broad rivers, transcontinental railroads have been built, factories have developed to mass produce cars and telephones, and human beings have been carried to the moon and back safely. The list of engineering achievements is huge, and the lessons taken from these successes are many.

Almost unconsciously society has looked to extend the lessons learned from these achievements to other areas of our lives. The use of these engineering (scientific) methods, heavily based on mathematical, predictable processes, however, has not been quite as successful in addressing the behaviors of human beings. And it is these humans who populate our organizations.

Looking at those steps and considering the people who will be participating during each of them reveals an important clue (please see figure 1).

The organization's leader and senior staff members are the most likely players in the change drama until it is time to execute the plan at the working level. Even though the line managers will probably receive some training as to the various aspects of the change before they are asked to begin implementation, they often are not participants in the early stages of the effort when the problem is initially defined and the plan for the solution developed. This will impact on them individually and collectively, in many cases by making line managers feel that they have no ownership in the final solution, only a work demand to execute the directions of higher authorities. This latter development challenges the establishment of *mutual purposes* between leaders and followers discussed earlier.

Steps for Change	Key Participants
Perception of crisis	Leader(s)
Gathering of data	Staff
Problem diagnosis	Leader/Senior Staff
Planning	Leader/Senior Staff
Plan implementation	Line Management
Evaluation	Leader/Senior Staff
Plan modification	Leader/Senior Staff

Figure 1. Participants in Steps for Change

To take this issue one step further, the other working members of the organization are even more removed from the change process and must depend upon communication from their supervisors or formally distributed information from the senior leaders.

Research has shown that each level of the organization usually has the most trust in those people with whom they interact on a regular basis. They, in effect, establish an understanding of their immediate environment that helps them to feel secure, to connect to the second level of Maslow's Hierarchy. The more removed from that immediate environment that other individuals are, the lower the trust level will often be. This is reflected in the stratified layers in most large organizations, but these divisions in trust and communications can exist even in small organizations where people do not regularly interact with each other.

Examined in light of our original definition of leadership, we are now operating in an atmosphere where mutual purposes may not yet exist, complicating the leadership problem. In addition, many organizational members may find their work security threatened by changes over which they sense they have no control. This may lead them, often instinctively and without conscious thought, to take actions to give them the internal feeling that they are regaining a sense of control over their immediate environment.

This response is resistance to change. It is real, it is common, and it can halt even worthwhile and needed changes. It may take the form of a planned work slowdown, lack of routine cooperation, or less concern about quality work performance—probably an almost infinite variety of human responses to a situation that is perceived to have a negative impact on the individual. It may drive individual as well collective responses such as strikes or organized work disruptions. In any case, the humans will intentionally not be implementing the planned changes as desired by the organization's leaders.

In addition there are often other subtle, covert actions that may impact negatively upon the intended new directions. The disruption of the social network that is imbedded in the culture may cause a variety of frustrations, sometimes interrupting the established communications patterns and preventing individuals from working effectively together. Stress may begin to rise within those affected, and the physiological impacts of that increase may have a variety of unpredictable impacts on workers, ranging from minor irritability to serious illnesses. The responses will be largely individual, often dependent on genetic and other factors not within the purview of the organization's leaders and often not consciously within the control of the individuals concerned.

The problem, then, is more complex than simply executing a well-designed plan in a step-by-step manner. A structured, engineering format will probably accurately reflect the steps needed to solve the *technical* aspects of the changes desired. However, a parallel plan must take into account the human actions and responses to those actions that will result because of the people who must effect the necessary changes. And the human aspects will be complicated further by the differences in personality types, backgrounds, life experiences, and perceptions as to the situation underway.

In summary, many organizational leaders who desire to make changes make an assumption that the change process will be a rational and linear series of steps when organizations—and the people who compose them—are often neither rational nor linear. The resultant resistance to change will be very individual in nature, deeply rooted psychologically, and not necessarily rational nor predictable. There are no precise, engineering solutions for addressing human behaviors.

> Any well-designed change effort should recognize that resistance to change must be addressed by actions that take into account the human responses by those who must effect the necessary changes.

As stated by Harvey Robbins and Michael Finley in their book *Why Change Doesn't Work*, "Visualizing the future is the venue of the right brain. But the task of actually constructing roads toward that vision of the future is the purview of the left." This would infer that the solution to the complex dilemma of establishing an effective *changing* methodology must lie in an *integration of methods*—a merging of the intuitive and sensing personality types, the rational and the irrational. But how can that be done?

7

The Solution

Before any solution can be developed, those engaged in guiding organizational change and those who study it must recognize that the current methodologies need improvement. There is no reason to accept a 30 percent success rate when it is likely that a much higher degree of success can be achieved.

Returning to the issue of change, it is not possible to continue doing the same things and expect a magical improvement. Having delved thus far into this subject, it is now assumed that the reader is open to suggestion. The admission of crisis is at hand.

Much data has been collected in the areas of change and change management, but much of it has been viewed in a piecemeal fashion. Over the past fifty years, many of the concepts noted earlier have been identified and tested successfully. However, the development of a general theory and related usable methodologies to guide practitioners of change has not been done effectively. Instead the method *de jour* has tended to prevail.

We saw Organizational Development emerge from some exceptionally productive research reported during the period 1930-1970. When that did not prove to be a universal solution and a new competitive threat to U.S business interests in the 1980s from Japan created a crisis, we moved to quality improvement as mirrored in Total Quality Management and some related quality enhancing methodologies. When the incremental improvement processes did not solve all problems, Business Process Engineering (BPR) emerged as a fix-all solution. Then reengineering caught on and executives and their consultants were reengineering everything from leadership to entire enterprises.

The one thing common to all these programs, however, was that they did not prove to be universally successful. The differences between private and public sector organizations, specific functional processes to be performed, existing organizational cultures, and even geographic location served to challenge the one-size-fits-all approach. There were many attempts to generalize, but often the jump was made from a limited number of successful cases to a universal solution without sound research to define the cases where a given approach would be most successful.

The solution, then, lies not in trying to apply any of the earlier-developed approaches to a new problem, but rather in developing ncw solutions by identifying (and developing as necessary) an appropriate unique methodology for each situation where significant change is needed.

There is a need to organize the field of data so that practitioners can easily and quickly assess the current situation, identify the desired final state, and then execute an effective plan. At this point it is not a significant variation from the step-by-step method cited in Chapter 6. But the devil is in the details, and it is *the execution of those steps* that needs to be changed. Most change efforts will pass through the same stages, but some additional steps may well enhance the final results.

However, before looking at any new steps, it is important to note that significant change will not take place if the organizational leaders do not take ownership of the change *process*. It is their job to establish a leadership relationship with the members of the organization who will follow, and to do so they must establish a sense of mutual benefit. If the leaders do not demonstrate—through their actions in completing the daily responsibilities of their positions—that they are committed to the changes required, they will send a message that they do not support the change process. Their espoused (spoken or written) beliefs will be in conflict with their demonstrated (behavioral) beliefs. When followers see this inconsistency, they will usually interpret *behaviors* as reflecting the true intentions of the leader.

> Significant change will not take place if the organizational leaders do not take ownership of the change process.

Once organizational leaders have established that changes are required, agree to fully support the change process and understand the requirements of the change effort, the actual change effort can proceed with a dual emphasis: one will involve the "technical" changes to environment, processes or structure while the other will address the "human" changes that must support them. First on the agenda of the latter will be to stop *resistance to change* before it can start. Impossible? Not really.

One way to look at an enhanced approach to leading change is to frame the process using the basic concepts suggested by Robert Blake and Jane Mouton (mentioned in Chapter 1). By dividing the change effort into two general categories, one that addresses the specific organizational tasks to be accomplished and one that guides the human aspects,

Perception of Crisis
Leader's Vision

Organizational Change Tasks	**Human Change Aspects**
Gathering of data	Strategy for Changing
Diagnosis of problem	Mutual benefit development
Planning	Communications plan
Plan implementation	Resistance reduction
Evaluation of results	Value assessment/adjustment
Plan modification	Rewards

Figure 2. Integration of Task & Relationship

a balance appropriate to the situation can be developed between the task and relationship issues. Figure 2 represents this new approach to changing.

As shown in this chart, the perception of a need for change and the leader's vision of the end state remain tasks for the leadership. However, to balance the basic organizational change tasks, the leaders would now develop a Strategy for Changing. This would take into account the need to develop a sense of mutual benefits for leaders and followers and a way to ensure that solid two-way communications are established at an early date. This latter aspect will help to ensure that the followers do not do too much "worst case analysis," which can create enhanced resistance. Consideration of the communications means should take place to augment the most common one-way, top-down form of impersonal communications that so often accompanies a change effort.

In almost all cases where an organization undergoes significant changes, resistance to change will occur. Although it may be impossible to accurately predict exactly what form it may take, leaders should assume that it will be present in one form or another. Any change plans, or should they be called *changing* plans, must address the most prevalent types of resistance. But before discussing a simple way to reduce the difficulties associated with this resistance, a suggestion by Kurt Lewin may be helpful.

One of the tools used by Lewin to discuss a variety of issues was the "force field." In the case of organizational change, he looked at an everyday organization as being composed of forces that could be represented by vectors, which can be pictured as arrows that possess direction and velocity (force). An organization that is not changing would be represented by a force field where the vectors for change and those opposing it are of equal force but of opposite directions, resulting in no movement.

Most standard change methodologies would have the leaders of the organization effect change by increasing the forces for change by actively directing new behaviors, publishing directives encouraging new ways of doing business, providing training for personnel needing new skills, or utilizing a variety of directive techniques. When this happens, the natural resistance to change will occur and can be represented by an increase in forces resisting change. Although the new changes may well be put into place, the forces for change may require a large commitment of resources that would be unnecessary if it were not for the resistance of the people of the organization.

Lewin suggested that perhaps it would be possible to reduce or even eliminate the resistance to change ***before*** commencing the actual technical changes. Using the force field analogy, the vectors resisting change would be decreased in force initially so that the forces for change would naturally move the organization in the desired new directions. This would, theoretically, require less effort be devoted to the human aspect of change and thereby accelerate the needed changes.

In terms of our leadership definition, this would establish at the earliest possible time in the change effort that the leaders and followers have *mutual purposes* for successfully accomplishing the changes. This sounds very easy, but it is an over simplification; however, neither is it extremely difficult. The ultimate solution does require an understanding of why humans resist changes as discussed in Chapter 4.

What every leader wants is for the followers to accept the new directions and move as rapidly as possible to put them in place. What the followers want is to have a sense of control over their immediate environment so as to sense the security of Maslow's second level of needs hierarchy. These are not mutually exclusive events.

The solution, then, is to rapidly establish that the leaders *and* followers are in agreement that the changes are to their mutual benefit—both taking ownership in effecting them. Since the leaders should have established their support of the changes before starting the change process, the key now is to get the followers (or at least the greater number of them) headed in the same direction. But how can this be done?

The magic of *participation* can do wonders for this effort. This does not mean that leaders must surrender the helm of the ship to the followers and hope for the best. It does mean that the followers must ***perceive*** that they can participate in the development of the plans to effect the changes if only to review and critique them ***before*** they are put in motion. They must develop an internalized feeling that the leaders honestly want followers to participate in the process as it unfolds.

If the followers feel energized to accept and participate in the changes, the resistance to change will be minimized if not lowered significantly. This will allow the forces for change to push the organization in the direction of the desired changes. Simple? Almost.

> Followers must perceive that they can participate actively in the development of the plans to effect the needed changes.

So how can this be done? Almost every major change effort requires some form of data collection and analysis before a plan for the implementation of the changes can be developed. Although the largest part of this analysis process can be completed by professional staff members (or the leaders themselves), they will probably not have perfect information. This provides an excellent opportunity for the rest of the organization to participate, if only in a somewhat structured manner. This participation can be in the form of structured interviews or, in the case of a large organization, by the use of surveys. Questions can be related to specific aspects of the proposed changes and to those relating to the environment within which the changes will occur.

The simple asking for help by the leaders of the followers can become an ownership development process. Specific comments by followers can provide necessary fine tuning of the change management structure, and leaders will have the opportunity to answer a variety of questions that may be worrying the followers, individually or as a group. This feedback can go beyond the data gathering (survey question) process; it can involve followers in the final analysis by asking them to review the desired directions as, reportedly, supported by the data collection and analysis processes. If this step is done openly and honestly, leaders and followers will have an opportunity to exchange their individual and collective thoughts as to best methods for effecting the changes.

The follower input will both improve the final plan and develop within the members of the organization a feeling of ownership of the elements of the change. Resistance to change can be substantially reduced, and the resources and time needed for the change effort can be likewise reduced.

> Resistance to change can be substantially reduced by follower feedback, accelerating the pace of change and reducing the associated costs.

Also, to provide a solid foundation for permanent change, any changing should include a careful evaluation of the organization's cultural and operational values. Since the systems that ultimately will govern the conduct of the organization's operations are (or are not) supported by these values, ensuring that changes accomplished are in concert with the final set of desired values is critical. Tasks to be completed should include a careful assessment of the existing values and an established path to imbed the desired, or final, set of values. To ignore this task places the longevity of the other changes at risk for failure.

Finally, some provision should be made for a form of *rewards* that can provide organizational members with a tangible means of recognizing the accomplishment of the change objectives and final vision. Although this may single out individuals for particular recognition, leaders should not forget that the change has involved all the organization's people, not just a few prominent ones. These rewards could include special opportunities for advancement, monetary awards, extra time off, or, an organization-wide party. Everyone should feel a sense of accomplishment when the new vision has been achieved, not just a few senior executives. After all, it is not easy to change a leopard's spots.

8

A Model for CHANGING

A simple methodology using change consultant support can demonstrate how this can be done in practice. The term “consultant” can include either internal or external help to guide the organization through this *changing* process. The consultant represents expert knowledge in the management of the change effort, not a specific person or professional business entity.

For the purpose of this sample methodology, we shall call the process to be described the “Sawtooth Technique” as the initiative will constantly shift back and forth between the organization undergoing change and the consultant. The net result is intended to be a significant reduction in resistance to change and an accelerated change effort. The methodology literally “cuts” through resistance to change, thereby allowing the forces for change to more effectively push the organization in the new directions.

The Sawtooth Technique (see Figure 3) begins when a consultant, external or internal, is asked to guide a major organizational changing process. The first step for the consultant is to gather as much organizational information available and to prepare for an initial interview with the organization's leaders. This first leader meeting has two major purposes: to gather additional specific information about the organization and the intended changes; and to ensure that the organization's leaders have the knowledge and desire to support the change effort. The latter review of leader support is critical as a poorly-conducted change effort can cause damage to organization performance as well as to the individual members of the organization. If the leaders are not serious about the changes proposed, the effort should stop until all are ready to proceed.

The leader-provided information should include a comprehensive list of anticipated changes such as proposed organizational structure modifications, new processes or technologies to be introduced, changes to existing personnel policies, and the desired final organizational situation when the change effort ends.

Organization Participation	Consultant Contribution
	1. Review of organization knowledge
2. Interview leader(s)	
	3. Review of leader meeting & prepare interview guide
4. Interview employees	
	5. Review interview data & prepare survey draft
6. Meet with interviewed employees	
	7. Finalize survey
8. Administer survey to large population	
	9. Complete preliminary survey analysis
10. Brief leader(s)	
	11. Prepare organization briefing of data
12. Present data to organization	
	13. Prepare final report
14. Brief leaders	

Figure 3. The Sawtooth Technique

(It would be advantageous that the consultant be provided with administrative support in contacting and meeting with the identified representative organization members for interviews.)

The consultant then reviews the information available and prepares an interviewing guide for the next step. This structured guide is not intended to limit the interview discussions, but rather it should provide some consistency from interviewee to interviewee. As individuals are interviewed, the guide may be tailored some, but some consistency in the interviews will promote more accurate data analysis in preparation for survey development. This initial interview process need not be extensive. For most organizations, even very large ones, eight to twelve interviews of about one hour in length will provide sufficient data to proceed to the next step.

Once these interviews are completed, the consultant will retreat to a quiet place to make some sense of the information at hand. An in-depth analysis is not required, but rather the data should serve to support survey questions to which other organizational members can reply. However, while this survey development process is underway, another aspect is already working to reduce the resistance to change. The interviewees, armed with the reason for their interviews (to help guide the change process), have returned to their normal work stations. Discussing with their immediate contemporaries the reason for their "absence," they are starting to inform the organization of its future and will undoubtedly be given some ideas by those in their immediate work areas.

After a draft survey is developed, the consultant meets again collectively with the organizational members who were previously interviewed. An overview of the data gathered is presented (without identifying specific sources in most cases) to give the audience a sense of closure on this part of the exercise; the employees give information of value and the consultant returns a product for them to examine. Some enlightening comments from those interviewed can be expected, aspects to consider as the survey draft is reviewed.

The organization members also review the draft survey for completeness and appropriate wording. (This latter aspect is particularly important as organizations often develop unique meanings for words used commonly in the workplace. Being unaware of these specific meanings may elicit unexpected results when the words are not used in their local sense.)

Having reviewed the survey, the consultant develops the final survey as corrected by the organizational members, who, returning to their work stations, pass along more information that continues the involvement of many of those who will need to address the forthcoming changes. In practice, these interviewees often fan the flames of anticipation that will increase survey participation.

Once ready, the survey is then given to the largest available population. This survey has three purposes: to gather information from a broad, representative organizational population; to improve reliability of the interview data; and to further involve the people who constitute the organization. At this point the latter aspect is probably the most important as this simple survey—that takes perhaps fifteen minutes to complete—has now given *all followers* a chance to begin establishing their ideas of what *mutual purposes* mean to them. This is the point at which implementation is well underway—before any aspects of the organization itself are actually undergoing the anticipated changes. It will be participation at this point that opens the door to significantly reducing the resistance to change and may actually increase the forces for change.

Once the surveys are completed and returned, the consultant must complete a preliminary analysis of the data collected. This analysis should include the data gathered previously via interviews to examine any changes. The merger of qualitative (interview) and quantitative (survey) data will also provide a much greater opportunity to generalize about the entire organization.

Once the preliminary survey analysis has been done, the consultant should meet with the organizational leaders to discuss the results to date. This not only prevents unpleasant surprises during the following steps, but leadership perspectives can be added to the overall analysis. After integrating this final perspective, the consultant prepares for a major presentation to the entire organization.

At a general meeting, the consultant now presents the survey and analysis to the entire organization. This may not be an easy aspect to accomplish because many organizations cannot stop working to have a meeting that includes all organizational personnel. Several incremental meetings may be necessary.

At any major gatherings, the consultant must remain open to additional suggestions from the floor and should use this opportunity to engage the audience in the final analysis. This open participation should send a message that everyone's questions and ideas will be respected, a key point in giving each individual the *perception* that he has some control over his part of the workplace. A further strengthening of the *mutual purposes* is possible here with the active participation of the organization's leaders.

The final steps of this process will be to prepare and then present a final report of the data collection effort to the organizational leaders. It should be noted that this effort is not designed to replace other information gathering efforts of other organizational members. It is, however, designed more to collect information from and involve the people most affected by the coming changes. As they contribute actively to the effort, they also should come to understand why the changes are necessary and how they will be involved in effecting them. This should dramatically reduce resistance to change and prepare the organization for the actual implementation of the more structural changes in technology, processes, and related environment.

This is not, however, the final step in addressing the human part of the change equation. As the organization begins the *changing* process, it may be of value to repeat all or part of the previously noted aspects.

For instance, performance assessment prior to change plan modifications may provide additional opportunities to gather data directly from organizational members while further building their participation (and ownership). There are many effective ways to continue using participation to reduce resistance to change—for example, employing cross-functional teams to develop prospective solutions and plans as the change efforts proceed.

> There are a variety of ways to continue using participation to reduce resistance to change and enhance change efforts.

It is important to note that the leopard has been asked to assist in changing his spots.

9

An Example of Success

Each organization that undergoes significant changes to address some currently challenging issues must be regarded as a unique case. The one-size-fits-all solutions of the past have consistently proven to be limited in producing successful changes across different types of organizations.

Examining one challenging long-term success may provide some clues as to ways to use the previously discussed methodology within a large to very large organization.

The key underlying aspect to overcoming or minimizing resistance to change is developing a participative (or a perception of a participative) approach to identifying needs, planning a new state, effecting the needed changes, assessing the success, and then making any needed adjustments. The Sawtooth Technique seeks to use the largest possible participation of organization members in addressing the change. This often means getting large numbers of employees together at one time to evaluate various program aspects to include final survey results. There are some physical and operational reasons that may limit the ability to gather large groups of people together at the same time. These are issues for each organization to address, but the following example may provide some ideas as to how to effect large-scale changes throughout a large, geographically challenging organization.

The example is a large U. S. Navy command with a headquarters on the west coast of the United States. Following the end of the Vietnam War, the source of manpower, the universal draft, ended. This required that the Navy closely examine its policies and environment to more effectively use the manpower at hand. With the volunteer approach to filling the manpower needs, the quality of working environment and the management of personnel already serving became very important. There was a need for a new approach to the *employee retention issue.*

The command in question developed a very effective solution to the retention equation that bore a close resemblance to the Sawtooth Technique. A consultant team from the command headquarters could visit any individual unit and provide assistance as needed. Armed with a field-tested survey for doing an initial evaluation of the local environment, the team helped an individual unit identify elements that could be improved, helped unit leaders develop the knowledge needed to manage the process of changing, and provided guidance to develop solutions tailored to meet the specific unit needs.

This was a fine solution for a few small units, but how was the commander of the entire organization of 55,000 people located geographically over one-half of the earth's surface going to make the needed changes occur throughout the organization? The answer lay within a strategic approach that used the specific improvement methods within an overall plan. Patience was a key element, and the organization was allowed to change in an evolutionary rather than revolutionary manner. Overall, the change occurred over several years, an eternity for some of the participants, but it was essential for the people who were changing *one person at a time*.

The overall organization had two major subdivisions: one involving six aircraft wings with fixed geographic headquarters where individual units were home-based; and the other one involving six aircraft carriers which deployed overseas periodically with members of the various wings onboard the ships.

The leaders at all levels of these organizations were at different stages in their recognition of the retention problems and the development of solutions. Some organizations were ready for change, others were not. Although headquarters personnel were well aware of the need for most of the units to improve their individual performance in this area, they chose not to manage by decree. They adopted the Kurt Lewin approach to lower resistance to change while allowing the units to change when they were individually ready.

The staff maintained a team that was capable of working with any size of command that asked for assistance, whether it be an aircraft carrier with 3,500 personnel attached or an individual aircraft squadron of several hundred personnel. They were ready to assist in response to a phone call whenever a unit indicated a desire to improve. They also did their best to advertise successes and make their services known to all units, but they did not dictate to the individual commands. The plan actually used a form of leadership discussed earlier in this book, wherein they worked to establish the mutual purpose of solving the retention problem rather than directing the changes from above.

Strategically, parts of the organization changed faster than others. Some command units were more ready for change than others, but as more and more units improved, their sister organizations took notice. As a large number of squadrons in one wing improved, the results were registered in the improvement of the wing or ship retention statistics, putting pressure on other wings and ships to do as well.

Without identifying the specific commands that had achieved superior results, the successes of the first to change sowed the seeds for those who followed. Rewards to the most successful further encouraged the changes and eventually the number of high-performing units developed a critical mass. At that point the various internal consultants asked the senior headquarters to document the processes they had been following; with that request some standard operating procedures were established in an open, participative conference and the new culture was now defined in writing.

This strategic approach to changing allowed each unit to change at its own pace, to perceive its own readiness to address the issues at hand. Although this was a military command, this same strategic viewpoint can be applied to any large organization. Within a corporation, various functional entities such as engineering, manufacturing, administration and the like may divide the business into units with different subcultures. These various functional divisions may have very different change needs and be at a variety of levels in terms of readiness for change. Some may face an immediate crisis, others may be stable and require little new to complete their responsibilities to the organization as a whole. An incremental change that allows the corporation to evolve slowly into a new and more effective organization makes sense. Everyone can change at his own pace.

There is a need to recognize, however, that some individuals and organizational entities will simply refuse to change. The occasions where a small part of the organization ignores the overall trend of change must be addressed separately, and the senior leaders need to be aware that this is likely to happen in a large, complex organization. Where the best of leadership techniques don't achieve the desired results, it may be necessary to change the affected unit leadership and use more directive means to bring the last few elements into alignment. (In these cases, a careful look at the personality types strongly resisting changes may provide some answers as to the reasons for the magnitude of the resistance. Some of us simply do not enjoy change regardless of the situation.)

> Some individuals and entities may simply refuse to change; they need to be addressed individually as appropriate.

Some leopards think their present spots are more than adequate. They will need special care and attention to effect an alteration.

10

Making It Happen

Before a successful change effort can begin, an organization's leaders must understand the dynamics of the process of changing. It is not enough for the leadership to know that change is necessary and to have an idea of the end state they desire to achieve. They must have a clear view of the field ahead so that they can see obstacles that may drive their good intentions off course. That is what this book is about—taking a good look at actually changing the organization.

Previous chapters have discussed the underlying factors that affect humans when they are faced with change. There followed a discussion of the problem of moving an organization into a new, desired state along with a sample methodology for building a more effective organization. However, those guiding the change process will need some resources to make this all come together. What are the critical skills needed to make this change process effective?

Busy senior executives have many responsibilities in maintaining the day-to-day activities of the organization; these tasks will not disappear during a period of change. Therefore, it may be helpful to have a permanently assigned change agent oversee the change dynamics once the change is underway. The selection of this individual (or team) to manage the change elements themselves will be quite important to the success of the evolution. Although this person can be a member of the existing organization, it may be wise to look to the outside for the needed expertise.

Most organizations do not have the luxury of having on staff all the experts they might ever need. First, it would be costly to have an almost infinite number of employees as the external environment constantly changes, influencing organizational needs. Secondly, many skills are only needed on an irregular basis, and the capabilities would be expensive to maintain when not required. In addition, many areas of knowledge require constant updates, making the maintenance of skills expensive whether used or not. The conclusion to be gained, then, is that most organizations will benefit by maintaining the most critical, or core, skills internally while obtaining other expertise needed infrequently from external sources when needed and cost effective.

In terms of organizational change, some of the needed knowledge areas might include facilitation, data collection and analysis, survey development, and interviewing. Various computer skills common in the workplace would be employed to support presentations, statistics, reports and communications. Educational background and experience in utilizing various organizational intervention techniques such as Organizational Development (OD), Total Quality Management (TQM), Enterprise Reengineering, or Business Process Reengineering (BPR) might be needed. Underlying these areas would be the fields of applied behavioral psychology, social psychology, industrial psychology, sociology, and a host of other academic disciplines.

In examining only the technique/model discussed in Chapter 8, the use of a custom-designed survey is a critical tool of a supporting consultant. The development and use of surveys requires significant knowledge of research methods to include knowing how to conduct effective interviews, analyze data collected to formulate question areas and then develop valid, reliable survey questions. These are not skills relevant to many positions within most organizations.

If this required knowledge is not an important, core organizational skill, it might be best acquired on an "as needed" basis. It is a strong argument for using consultants who possess the specialized knowledge needed to build an effective change effort. Very large organizations undergoing significant changes over a long period of time might choose to develop internal consultants for a variety of reasons to include greater control of needed actions, reduced long-term costs, business security, or use of existing organizational knowledge. These reasons compete with external consultants who can bring to the table a fresh perspective along with experience working with a variety of similar (and dissimilar) organizations. The decision to employ internal or external consultants is, therefore, an important decision that is unique to each organizational entity.

Regardless of the choice of consultant source, however, the organization's leaders must be careful to remember that they, not the consultants, are leading the change effort. Consultants will eventually go away, whether to another job assignment within the organization or to consulting externally. The organization's leaders will need to maintain the change initiatives after the consultants have helped with the technical aspects and, hopefully, will continue to guide the organization in the future.

If these leaders surrender the leadership initiative to consultants, they will often struggle to regain their position relative to the followers once the consultants depart. This may affect not only the success of the change effort but also other areas where the leaders provide the overall guidance.

In addition, effective leaders have an established relationship with the followers prior to any needed changes. This relationship can help to communicate the need for change. If consultants are leading the organization in one direction and the established organizational leaders are indicating a different direction, followers will need to make a choice as to the sincerity of the leader's change support. Lack of line management actions to support the change effort may result, stopping needed change aspects before they can start to be effective.

The conclusions from this short discussion are as follow:

- Consultants, regardless of internal or external source, can assist an organization to change by contributing critical knowledge and skills to the effort.
- Leaders must understand the change process and use consultant-provided knowledge in an appropriate manner while maintaining their own leadership relationships with followers.
- Leaders' actions will help to signal support of consultant contributions and must remain in concert with the desired directions.
- Leaders must never surrender their leadership roles to consultants or they risk a long-term erosion of their regular positions of leadership.

> Leaders must understand the change process underway and maintain their regular leadership roles throughout a changing effort.

11

Last Thoughts

Changing large organizations is not brain surgery. It is more complex than that because many brains are involved, the brains of all the people in the entire organization. It is not a precise target that can be addressed with engineering style solutions, and it will remain somewhat an art as long as people are involved.

Leadership will be involved since the senior executives in the organization are likely to be the first to recognize the need to change and the desired end state, while it is the people of the organization who must do most of the changing. People are involved and any plans that are developed must account for the huge diversity that exists within any organization.

The changing process does not begin when the final plan for changes is executed; it begins as soon as the need for change is perceived by the leaders. The implementation stage of the change process is merely a change in intensity. Changing is already underway, and resistance to change is likely already in place. It is simply a *matter of degree* for both.

The ideas proposed are designed to do several things. It is important to keep them in mind when undertaking a large-scale change that:

- Leaders must understand the dynamics of changing and the impact of the changes proposed on others (stress).
- There are really two elements underway when a large-scale change is in motion: (1) the changes in structures, technologies and procedures of the organization and (2) the changes in behaviors of the people, which will then modify the culture over time.
- Resistance to change may be best addressed before it develops, allowing the forces for change to advance with less effort. Resistance to change is a normal response to changes in the environment where individual security is threatened by a perceived loss of control. It

should always be anticipated as an important factor in large organizational changes.

- There is no magic formula to effect change that will work for all organizations. The recipe for each will be different and should be tailored for their specific needs.
- Although consultant assistance from outside the organization may be valuable in effecting the needed changes, the leaders must never surrender the initiative to "outsiders." The day will come when the job is finished and the consultants will go away; the organization leaders will remain in charge.
- Organizations are populated with people. To change an organization, people must change, and they will change one person at a time.
- There are tools and skills that can assist the change leaders in reducing resistance to change and making the change occur more effectively (and efficiently).
- Human perceptions are important and will vary with each individual. Leaders must be aware that their perceptions may differ from others within the organization.
- Changing any large organization will demand knowledge of a diverse collection of leadership and management theories and techniques. This

is a strong argument for the continuing education of both leaders and followers in the modern environment.

The leopard will thank you sincerely for the new spots.

Acknowledgements

I wish to thank my parents, Port and Edith Martin, for starting me on a lifetime learning expedition and my sister, Mary Eagon, for tolerating a big brother during her formative years.

Most recently my wife, Gayle, has endured my hours of reading, thinking, and tinkering with the text of this book while giving me quiet and warm encouragement. Our children, Michael, Theresa, and Erik may someday benefit from the thoughts expressed here as they pursue their respective careers.

I must thank those men and women who have crossed paths with me and taught me so much: teachers, students, friends, relatives, coworkers, leaders, and followers. I also owe sincere gratitude to those who have written down their thoughts on similar subjects, and some of the most important ones have been mentioned in this book.

I must thank my editor, Karyn Wilkening, who made me rethink many a word and punctuation mark, and the publishing staff who have made this physical volume possible. Any errors that have survived are my responsibility.

References (Some Books Worth Reading)

Andrews, D.C. & Stalick, S.K. (1994). *Business Reengineering: The Survival Guide.* Englewood Cliffs, N.J.: Prentice- Hall.

Bennis, W. G. (1966). *Changing Organizations.* New York: McGraw-Hill.

Blake, R.R. & Mouton, J.S. (1972). *The Managerial Grid: Key Orientations for Achieving Production Through People.* Houston, TX: Gulf Publishing.

Conner, D.R. (1993). *Managing at the Speed of Change: How Resilient Mangers Succeed and Prosper Where Others Fail.* New York: Villard.

Hutchin, N.L. "Thriving on Change." *Enterprise Reengineering*, January/February 1996.

Kanter, R.M. (1983). *The Change Masters: Innovation & Entrepreneurship in the American Corporation.* New York: Simon & Schuster.

Keirsey, D. (1998). *Please Understand Me II: Temperment, Character, Intelligence.* Del Mar, CA: Prometheus Nemesis.

Kouzes, J. M. & Posner, B. Z. (1993). *Credibility: How Leaders Gain and Lose It, Why People Demand It*. San Francisco, CA: Jossey-Bass.

Kotter, J.P. (1990). *A Force for Change: How Leadership Differs From Management*. New York: The Free Press.

Kotter, J.P. & Cohen, D.S. (2002). *The Heart of Change: Real-Life Stories of How People Change Their Organizations.* Boston, MA: Harvard Business School.

Kotter, J.R. & Heskett, J.L. (1992). *Corporate Culture and Performance.* New York: The Free Press.

Kroger, O. & Thuesen, J.M. (1992). *Type Talk at Work: How the 16 Personality Types Determine Your Success on the Job*. New York: Delacorte.

Rost, J. C. (1991). *Leadership for the Twenty-First Century*. New York: Praeger.

Schein, E.H. (1992). *Organizational Culture and Leadership* (2nd Ed.). San Francisco, CA: Jossey-Bass.

Made in the USA